Yellow

Danny Strack

www.dannystrack.com

INSTRUCTIONS

Read all instructions before doing anything.

Section headers (other than this one) are mostly jokes.

The **Real Table of Contents** is buried in the **Ingredients**, at the bottom of the **Nutritional Facts** table.

<u>These poems are intended to be recited out loud.</u> For each poem, close your eyes and picture Dny saying it at you in his various voices. For best results, memorize all poems.

The second voice in "Texas Tea" should be high-pitched. "An Open Letter to Humans" should read with a high-class British accent. "Songasm" should morph into a song. "And Now, A Song" is a song the whole way through. The lines about North Carolina and Texas in "Accents of the South" should be read in alternating North Carolina and Texas accents.

Stand up and say, "I am the best at following instructions," aloud.

Use MS PowerPoint to draw a picture of a turtle, and send it to the following address, along with a self-addressed / stamped return envelope:

Danny Strack
401 N. Pleasant Valley Rd.
Austin, TX 78702

... and we will let you know within 6-8 weeks whether you have been accepted into the DNY School of PowerPoint Art.

Now that you've read all of the instructions, ignore all of the physical actions listed above, sign your name at the top of the page, then put your pencil down on your desk and sit quietly until any other students in the room are done.

You are an ace at reading instructions!

CONTENT TABLE

DEDICATION

I will reach the top no matter the personal cost to my body!

Dedicated to:

Texas

...and the rest of the United States of America.

Nutrition Facts

Serving Size: ~2 Pages
Servings Per Container: 26

Average Amount Per Serving:

Calories: 30
Jokes: 4.84
Funny Jokes: 1.96
Unfunny Jokes: 0.93
Laughter from Jokes: 2
Calories Burned by Laughter: 5

Sadness: 1
Cognitive Dissonance: Δ
Metaphors: 1.32
Central Metaphors: 12
Similes: 9
Fake Advertisements: 0.76

Vitamin A.................. 10%
Vitamin C.................. 0%

Riboflavin...... What is Riboflavin?
Fat.............. 0%*

Ingredients:

Paper/Cardboard (Plant Cellulose, Hemi-Cellulose, Clay, Fillers),
Artificial Colors (Black #1, Yellow #5, Cyan #2, Red #6),
Glue (Bone/Hide/Scraps, Water, Lime, Hydrochloric Acid, Phosphoric Acid),
Yellow

May Contain Trace Amounts of: Cheez-its.

Definitely Contains Large Amounts of Thanks to All the Proof Readers!!!
Extra Special Thanks to Robby Cale & Teresa Johnson for Edits

*Okay. I mean... maybe there's a little fat. As a word chef, I do my best to avoid putting fat into my work, but if we're being honest, a little fat is unavoidable, right? It just makes the text tastier, right?

I don't want to toot my own horn.
May I please borrow your sousaphone?

I just got one of those automatic self-driving cars.
They are very intuitive.
You don't even need a manual.

Is my turn signal broken?
Nope!
Everyone is just an asshole.

TEXAS TEA

$1.79 for gas.

That is so cheap I want to pour it all over my body,
slather it on like sunscreen.
I think I want to make a slip-n-slide with gasoline.

I'm gonna fill up my electric car.
I'm gonna fill the frame of my bicycle.

Won't that just make it heavier?

Yeah, but it's so cheap...
I wanna start using it as a condiment,
slap it on my sandwich like mayonnaise...
I wanna use it as a glaze on my Easter ham!

Gol'damn!

That's so cheap I wanna start drinking it!
Move over Long Island Iced Tea!
Gimme some Texas Tea!

Hooooooowee!

That's cheaper than two liters of clean water at the same station!

I'm used to only seeing this number grow!
Holy frak! How did it get so low?

Well holy frak, they fracked the holes.

What does that mean?

It's not that complicated.

Here in America, we had all this oil that was too deep underground to get to
with traditional drilling methods.

So, we came up with a new technique called "hydraulic fracturing,"
or... "fracking,"
which is where they take clean water,
mix it with toxic chemicals,
and then pump the mixture underground so it forces the oil out!

8

They leave most of the toxic stuff underground to contaminate the drinking water and soil, but that doesn't matter 'cause now... we've got all this oil!

Just... so much oil I'm gonna use it to deep fry my turkey this year.
So much oil we're gonna need America's whole breadbasket to sop it up.

So anyways, OPEC,
                              the Organization of Petroleum Exporting Countries!
Right.
They saw that America had all this oil,
so they're maintaining high production,
which is artificially reducing the price of oil.

And that's why a gallon of gas suddenly costs the same as a grande coffee from Starbucks,
or half a venti mocha from Starbucks,
or a third of a bag of ground roast beans from Starbucks.
I'm just saying,
Starbucks coffee is unreasonably expensive.
Yet gas is surprisingly cheap right now!

Which is great!
You know what's not great?
We didn't used to have earthquakes in Texas or Oklahoma.
We started fracking, and guess what?
Earthquakes throughout Texas and Oklahoma,
every year since.

What's not great is oil barons stealing back the shitty land we gave the Native Americans so they can profit from ruining it.

What's not great is flammable tap water in homes too close to fracking sites.
Thousands of Americans with cancer from living too close to fracking sites.

Anyways, fracking is where you take clean water and trade it for cheap gas.

And now you can buy gas for less than a liter of water at that same station.

AN OPEN LETTER TO HUMANS

I scratch these words into a rock in the hopes of reaching you through the ages.
I do not know if the words or the rock will last through the millennia,
but I have no other medium of communication.
I only hope that my words stand the test of time better than my people.

I am writing to you in Rexian, the language of the T-Rex...
which is what I am.

I realize you probably do not speak Rexian
and may mistake these words for random scratch marks on the rock.

Actually getting this open letter to you is a very frustrating dilemma, which I do not
know how to solve.

But I must persist.
Though we are separated by time, space, language barriers and the limitations of my
walnut-sized brain,
it is vital that I find a way to bridge these gaps.

Despite all the differences, your people are not so very different than my own:
We are both going extinct.

Technically, in my case, it has already happened.
There was nothing we could do about the environmental collapse that caused our
extinction.
Faced with asteroid impacts, massive volcanic activity, and dropping temperatures and
sea levels,
the best our T-Rex scientists could come up with was inventing the bifocals.

It was out of our hands.
Our tiny, tiny hands.

But you have big hands.
Proportionally to your body size.

And yet, although there is still time to save yourselves,
you seem hell-bent on seeing this thing through.

For your people,
faced with the environmental impact of massive human activity resulting in rising
temperatures and sea levels,
your scientists are telling you exactly what to do,
and yet your politicians,
who are supposed to represent the will of the people,
are doing nothing about it.

It's like you are hurling the asteroid at yourselves.

I'm not sure who I pity more:
myself, who is already dead,
or you who can see it coming,
know what needs to be done,
but are unwilling to do it.

Killing yourselves and so many other higher-level life forms at the same time...
And you call us cold-blooded!

I also find it a strange twist of fate that the burning of fossil fuels made from myself
and my dead relatives is the very source of the environmental collapse you now face.

So if you won't believe your scientists,
perhaps you can take it from a lower life form:
Just pretend CO_2 is an asteroid if it makes it easier.
You should really do something about that asteroid.

Sincerely yours,
Dr. Nigel T. Rex, III

A TIP FOR TRICK OR TREATERS

The crappiest masks are made of hard plastic.
They don't stretch like expressive rubber masks;
they just kind of sit on your face, unnatural and unmoving.

Like that island of waste floating on the Pacific Ocean,
twice the size of Texas and mostly made of plastic.

We call it the great garbage patch,
but really it's just a big plastic mask the size of Europe,
planted in the ocean, unnatural and basically never going to biodegrade.

In the great garbage patch,
we've dressed up the fish in cheap swim fins,
and slapped frozen joke store smiles onto microorganisms.

We're cellophaning our food chain,
and as the island grows,
we won't even be able to recognize our own insides soon.

They'll be all wrapped up in plastic.

IT'S THE GREAT PLASTIC, CHARLIE BROWN!

Hey blockhead!

Have you heard about the great garbage patch?
It's really great.

Every year on Halloween,
the Great Plastic rises up out of the garbage patch he judges to be most sincere.

So instead of trick-or-treating this year,
I'm going out to the garbage patch,
and if I sit there long enough,
I'll see the Great Plastic with my own eyes.

And he's gotta pick this one. He's got to.
I don't see how a garbage patch could be more sincere than this.

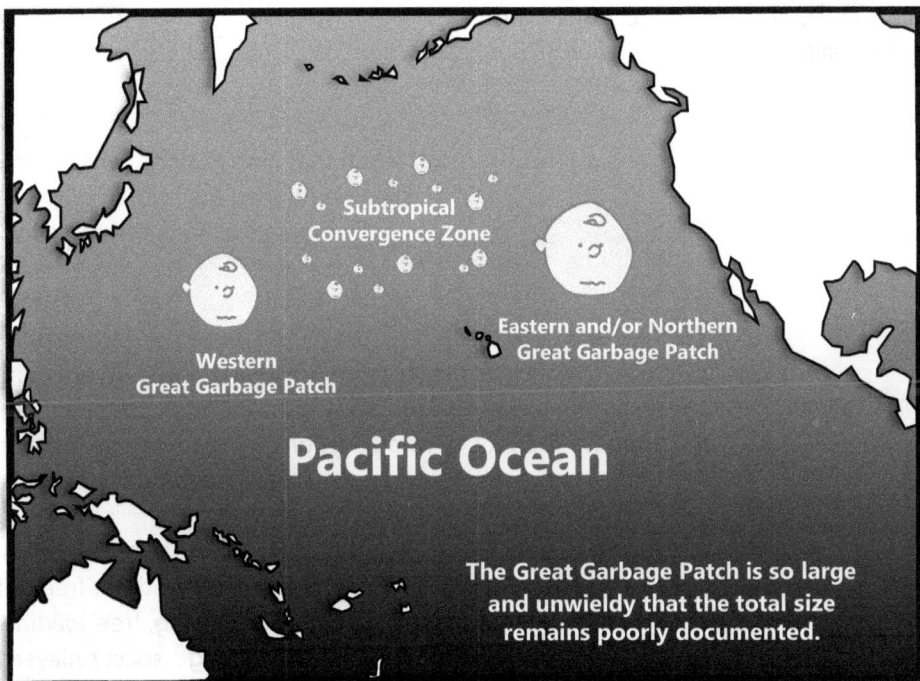

Subtropical Convergence Zone

Western Great Garbage Patch

Eastern and/or Northern Great Garbage Patch

Pacific Ocean

The Great Garbage Patch is so large and unwieldy that the total size remains poorly documented.

POLITICAL THEATER 2016

When a far-left liberal views the world through blue tinted glasses...
Republicans all look the same.

They'll always be the ones to blame!
Religio-nuts!
Denying the science behind global warming,
while embracing the science of global war and oil refining.
They want to give automatic machine guns and grenades to kids,
so they can kill all the Muslims and Mexicans
coming into the country
and taking jobs they wouldn't have worked anyway,
then arrest everybody, try them as adults,
and put them to work in industrialized jails!

They want Obama to fail,
and Hillary to die.
They want every cop in riot gear!
And they pray every day to Jesus Christ...
and Donald Trump!

But when that always-right conservative
slips on his own rose tinted glasses...
Democrats all look the same too.

Whew!
Unrealistic!
Atheistic flip-floppers who can't agree on anything
but taking away guns and defense spending,
and pumping the money into abortions for married trans-triads,
and health care for trees!

They want Syrian refugees sleeping on all our couches,
so they can enact terrorist plots to hand out free pot
that will turn all our kids into free-loving, free-loading,
free-rangin', freedom-hating... soccer players!

And if our country was a movie theatre,

most our politicians   would   sit in the thin wings.

While the rest of us would occupy the wide stripe in the middle,
with the best view of the action,
only we can't hear the soundtrack running
under the shouting match between left and right:

Dueling with one-sided debates!

They can't even hear their own arguments,
'cause their heads have been shoved up their asses
so long...
that shit...
is now full of them.

Political discussion in America is politically disgusting.
The debate's been taken over by extremists:
News programs populated by pretty people repeating talking points,
news stories calculated to get ratings rather than report,
and if I wanted to watch someone lip synch meaningless shit,
I'd turn to BuzzFeed and learn the nine surprising ways Justin Bieber drank himself
under the tabloids last week.
But if I want the real news,
I flip to someone like John Oliver or Larry Wilmore,
like the truth has turned so tainted,
we can't take it without a joke to help it go down.
Like the truth is a prop in a complicated magic trick,
and we're all so mesmerized by the wizard's hands,
we don't notice the mirrors turning 3D scenes into 2D images.

And that's what's wrong with extremists:
They only see one flat side of a world in three dimensions,
like someone forgot to hand them their 3D glasses.

And if you want to watch the movie without getting a splitting headache,
your glasses need one red lens and one blue lens...

Otherwise you can't see
what's really happening.

THE POLITICAL SCIENTIFIC METHOD

The scientific method is: Question, Hypothesis, Prediction, Testing, Analysis.

Question: Why don't conservative politicians believe in climate change?

Hypothesis: They don't understand the basic science behind it.

Prediction: They secretly do understand the science, but can't see the ramifications 'cause they're BLINDED BY GOLD!

Testing: An exhaustive study of voting records and campaign speeches shows it's actually about 50/50.
Half of them really don't understand the basic science.
The other half are hypocritical sycophants more interested in their bank accounts and stock holdings than in the well-being of American citizens,
a.k.a., "BLINDED BY GOLD!!!"

Analysis: It's easy to think conservatives don't believe in science, but they're just running a different experiment...
They're using the political scientific method.

It's pretty cynical.

Cynical Question: Can we get people to vote for us, even though our policies are against their self-interest?

Cynical Hypothesis: Yes! We'll do it through a combination of strawmen and smoke screens.
We'll weaponize fear and wage a social media war campaign based on class, claiming to be the party of economic responsibility,
while secretly being responsible for the debt and the deficit, and the widening wage gap,
but they won't see it 'cause we'll talk about outdated economic concepts, comparing everything else to communism and Islam.

We'll glorify guns while ignoring gun violence, and say immigrants are the enemy...
surely not big business...
and not us...

We'll remind them of good ol' days that never existed,
making them to forget they now live like princes.
We'll tell them we're good Christians while we ignore the sick and poor.

We'll pit them against each other on the basis of race instead of economics.
We'll trick them into confounding color, class and character till they can't tell the
difference!

Cynical Prediction: There's no way the American public will fall for it.

Cynical Testing: Nope! Turns out they do!
Watch as we parade out candidates like Donald Trump,
and they turn out in droves and vote and cheer!

Cynical Analysis: Winning an election is easy if you throw enough money at it.

Cynics just don't want anyone to apply scientific ideas idealistically.

Idealistic Question: Will we average people ever see through the smoke and
dollar signs and enact real world change on issues like class, social justice and the
environment?

Idealistic Hypothesis: Yes, and we're already starting to see cracks of light.
For every Kim Davis there's a Wendy Davis.
For every Trump, there's a Sanders and a Clinton.
For every Palin there's a Fey.

There will be a day when we stop fearing each other.
When we see the real monsters.
When we focus on real truths.
Even the pope seems to be on our side.
Fascist ideals will eventually die.

Idealistic Prediction: I have my doubts, but I choose to believe.

Idealistic Testing: Currently in progress.

Idealistic Analysis: To come.

THE ARMS RACE (OF JACKSON AND GEORGE)

Jackson wanted bigger muscles.
He was tired of losing arm-wrestling contests to his friend, George,
who was quite buff.

George said Jackson should join him at the gym,
but Jackson wasn't into that...
Jackson had a master's degree in biomedical engineering from Duke University!
And he enlisted some quick genetic engineering,
and replaced his human arms with the arms of a grizzly bear,
which, as you know, can lift half a ton of salmon.
And he challenged George to an arm-wrestling match!

It was no contest.
Jackson won three out of three and left claw marks in the back of George's hand.

George was not to be outdone.
He was also interested in genetic engineering,
having obtained his PhD from John Hopkins with an emphasis on biochem,
while going to bartending school at night.

So George got himself a pair of gorilla arms,
which, as you know, can lift over two tons of salmon.
And not only did this move multiply his bartending skills by ten,
but he also swept all three sets when he arm-wrestled with Jackson.

So Jackson replaced his arms with sharks!
Not shark fins,
but literally sharks,
which, as you know, have mouths for hands!
And the next time they had an arm-wrestling match,
Jackson's shark arms bit George's gorilla arms clean off!

Now George was pissed,
so he said, "Screw genetic engineering,
I want some good ol' regular engineering!"

So he replaced his arms with automatic machine guns,
and he broke a lot of bottles,

but he also killed Jackson's shark arms while saying something like,
"How do you like these guns?"

And Jackson was like, "Fuck that!"
And he replaced his arms with two nuclear bombs!

Now at this point,
I want to pause the story,
to take an reader poll.

Setting aside the fact that this sounds fucking badass,
raise your hand
if you literally think it would be okay for an average citizen to have nuclear bombs
in the real world.

I'm hoping this is a small minority.

And if you didn't raise your hand,
then you agree that an average citizen doesn't have the right to own a nuclear
weapon.

Therefore, you agree that our constitutional right to bear arms should be limited
at some level.
Now we just have to agree where that level is.

So anyways, back to the story,
Jackson had nuclear weapons for arms,
and George was like, "Whoa!"
And Jackson was like, "What? I've got a dead-man switch!"

And George said, "Maybe we let this arms race get a little out of hand."
And Jackson said, "You're right, maybe we should both just go back to grizzly
bear arms."
And George said, "You're right, those were pretty badass too."

So they both went back to regular-sized bear arms,
which were more than enough to impress their friends, slay their enemies,
and play to a tie every time they arm-wrestled.

Jackson and George
School of Genetic Engineering, Mixology and Arm-Wrestling

Have you ever wanted to learn how to splice human DNA with animal DNA at night, in a laid back, comfortable environment?

Join professors Jackson and George for late afternoon classes in advanced mixology. Then enjoy the dinnertime entertainment as your professors spar in their favorite pastime - arm-wrestling.

After dinner and games, the real fun begins, with cocktails and highly technical lectures every night from midnight till four a.m., led by the winner of the arm-wrestling contest. Be sure to bring your notebooks!

Then at four, the whole party moves to the lab for the after-party and live subject testing. If you're one of the lucky few chosen to be experimented on, you just might end up with an animal's body part spliced onto your body! So cool!

Why would you get a tattoo of a dragon on your arm, when you could turn your whole arm into a dragon!? Realize these dreams and more
with Jackson and George! *

* "highly credentialed"

AT WAR

My cat,
Franny,
is at war... with everything.

She fights things she's supposed to fight,
like cat toys, roaches and rats.
But she also scratches the other cats,
they all have claw marks on their backs...
And she bites at feet and the hands that feed her,
she likes to attack trees and rocks and the air,
and feels a need to mark her territory is everywhere.
Sometimes I think she's at war with ideas,
with good sense and decency...
she certainly walks around naked all the time showing her butthole to
everybody...
I think she's at war with the entire world...

She reminds me of America.

Like how we're in a trade war with China,
a cold war with N. Korea,
and shirtless posing war with Russia.

We're at war in Iraq, Syria and Afghanistan,
but we aren't actually at war with those countries.
We're really at war with Isis, Al Qaeda, the Taliban,
and any other extremists that happen to live anywhere,
as well as other places, where, we are also at war with them.

Because we're at war with terror,
the idea of fear itself.

In fact,
our government has declared war with tons of other things you can't really attack,
like drugs, illiteracy and childhood obesity.
In our country, there's a war on Christmas,
the middle class,
carbon and the temperature.

And when I look at Franny, I say,
"You have to relax, cat!
Just sit on my lap and let me pet you!
Please calm down.
Why do you have to pee on everything?

Instead of raising your tail to spray,
why can't you raise a peace sign?"
But every time Franny holds up her fingers,
she's got her claws out.

She reminds me of America.

I think we need to stop peeing everywhere.
There's no need to mark our territory anymore.

I think we should declare war on war,
or maybe...
rather than pissing again on things we already pissed on,
let's just declare peace.

Let's start with peace in Congress.
Enroll our House Reps in relationship counseling,
and have Senators take classes in compromise.
We'll send flowers to Harry Reid and secretly sign them from Mitch McConnell.

And once that's done,
we'll have them withdraw troops from the Middle East
and send children's choirs instead.

Let's stop all pissing on the environment.
May conservatives become conservationists.

Let's find peaceful solutions for prejudice,
let's tell terror we don't fear it,
may we make peace with drugs and the middle class.

May we make peace with ourselves,
with our war-making nature.

Even Franny is growing up.
She isn't so angry all the time.

She seems a lot happier basking in the sun than fighting invisible enemies.

And last night she personally groomed my beard for, like, ten minutes straight.
It was the best feeling ever.

23

A MOMENT OF NOISE

In the wake of each wave of gun violence crashing,
it is easy to be overcome
by the fragility of human life.
To be paralyzed by fear
for our lives and the lives of those we love.
To be pulled under by all that salt water.

Whether the target was
a school in Columbine,
a church in Charleston
or a nightclub in Orlando,

We struggle to understand the madness that motivates a shooter.
Seeing everything by new light,
we want to reach out to everyone affected.
But our arms are not long enough.
So instead we gather locally
and do our best.

We ask for moments of silence
to remember the dead.
                  Silence,
                          in solidarity with the grieving.
Silence,
      in recognition of
             what happened.

And I respect this tradition.
But so far, these moments don't seem to be working.
Silence is excellent for reflecting on problems,
but does little to prevent them.

Meditation alone isn't enough anymore.

So yes,
let's have a moment of silence,
but then,
let's have a moment of NOISE.

A moment for action.
Let's take a moment to join a movement.

Even if we're collectively only snapped out of complacency for a few seconds,
we could start up a song in those moments.
A song of support for everyone affected.

A chorus of
                No: we do not consent to be killed by your random acts of hate,
        No: we will not give in to fear.

We will rumble till the bigots can hear us.
        Until the gun lobby can hear us.
                Until all the terrorists can hear us.

We will not go gentle.
        We will not say nothing.
                We will not be quiet.
                Anymore.

When someone falls overboard,
you make a noise and throw them a raft.

Our boat is lilting and keeling in a storm of bullets.
People are flying over the rails.

People of America.
I ask you all now,
        for a moment
                        of
                        noise.

THE DEFINITION OF A TERRORIST

"Muslim" is not a synonym for "Terrorist."

A lot of folks seem to think it is.
Like they heard the term "Muslim Extremist,"
and thought it meant anyone who is extremely Muslim.

When even that term, "Muslim Extremist," is unfair on the surface.
This would imply that we're not just at war with Muslims who are extreme...
ly violent, but also also at war with Muslims who are extreme...
ly – nice,
extreme... ly – good singers,
extremely – into Star Wars trivia,
extremely – white 'cause they converted from Christianity late in life,
extremely – tired of being accused of being terrorists.

So if we aren't at war with Muslims,
how do we know what a terrorist looks like?

Well... most mass shootings are carried out by white men,
young dudes with racist chips off the old blocks on their shoulders.
The majority of bombs dropped throughout history were triggered by hairy white
hands like these.

When you're in airport security trying to pick the potential bomber out of line,
don't bother with the poor guy already getting a hard time from TSA,
but narrow your eyes instead at the Aryan with a little stubble and the camo
hunting cap you thought was ironic.
Most modern American terrorists look like Tim McVeigh,
Ammon Bundy and Dylann Roof.
The truth is most terrorists look like me.
Like the guy sitting next to you.
They look like Dick Cheney's high school yearbook picture,
like young clones of Donald Trump.
In fact... they look exactly like Donald Trump.

Last summer,
a friend visiting from Egypt got quiet and asked what I thought of Trump.
Her tone was so ominous.

I laughed and said,
"He definitely won't be the nominee.
He's a joke!
Most of us don't really believe that stuff.
Certainly not the majority.
Please don't judge my people based on the words and actions of just a few bad
men."

Then he won the primaries.
I grew so embarrassed for my country.
And when he won the presidency
my embarrassment turned into fear,
into outright terror, we as a nation could ever make a mistake like this.

So if you need an example of what an American terrorist looks like,
of someone threatening violence in pursuit of political goals,
just look at Donald Trump!

And if you were to ask an average, extremely nice, normal, pitch-perfect,
Wookie-obsessed Muslim what they thought of the Jihadists,
of Isis and their leaders,
they might laugh it off and say,
"Oh, most of us don't really believe that stuff.
Certainly not the majority.
Please don't judge our people based on the words and actions of just a few bad
men."

TRUMP REFLECTS ON PHYSICS

Donald Trump steps out of the shower,
looks in the mirror,
and likes what he sees.

Trump sees a man aged by experience.
A man who picked himself up by his own bootstraps to rise to the top of an
empire.
Who built a fortune, lost it, regained it,
became a financial mogul, a celebrity, and now,
the President of the United States.

Trump thinks he's pretty smart.
Trump is in on all the jokes about his hair.

The look just makes him memorable.
Trump knows that all tweets are good tweets –
you just have to walk the fine line between Katy Perry and Mel Gibson...
and even Mel is making a comeback, so who knows?

Trump nods to himself and smiles.
Trump knows how to please his constituency.

But then Trump frowns.
Because... Trump still hasn't worked out how to please the people who aren't his
constituency...

Trump never understood why these people couldn't pick themselves up by their
bootstraps like Trump did. Like Trump did twice!

Trump always thought they must be stupid or bad.

But at that moment,
Trump has an epiphany unlike any Trump has ever had before.

Trump is thinking about physics.

Trump suddenly realizes:
it is literally impossible to pick yourself up by your own bootstraps.

Trump precariously stands on one foot and pulls up on his toes.

Gravity won't allow it.

Trump realizes that a person physically cannot rise without a hand up,
without shoulders to stand on,
or at least a rope ladder descending from the ceiling.

Trump's head is spinning,
Trump suddenly realizes that nearly half the world will never own a pair of boots,
maybe not even a pair of shoes.

Trump remembers the millions he inherited from his father,
and in that moment he even wakes to what it means to be a white man in
America... and the full weight of his life's privilege comes crashing down
on his now slumped shoulders.

Trump realizes there never were any bootstraps,
that he hasn't been in on the joke at all!
Trump see how offensive his views had been!
Trump hasn't been walking a fine line at all...
He's been outright racist!
Trump has to tell everybody he was wrong,
damn his constituency,
Trump is switching sides,
Trump will be a good man after all!

And in his excitement Trump slips on his bathmat
and bangs his head on the edge of his Olympic-class whirlpool toilet.

Not too bad,
a small bump,
there's no blood or anything.
Just a minor concussion and bit of short term amnesia.

Trump forgets all about physics.
Trump has no memory of the last few minutes at all.
And after standing back up,
Trump doesn't even realize that he ever fell.

A BOAT

Over 40 years ago, the Supreme Court issued their decision in Roe versus Wade:
Finding for Roe,
legalizing abortion during the first trimester,
and leaving the decision in the hands of the mother.

The conservative side of the land hasn't rested a second since in trying to
overturn this decision.

There's this Christian joke about a man of faith
who climbs on top of his house to avoid a flood.

As the waters rise, his friends float by in a boat and offer him a lift.
"No thanks," he says, "God will save me."

Eventually, the man drowns.
He ascends to heaven and goes before God and says,
"What the hell? I thought you were going to save me!"

And God says,
"Yeah, I sent you that boat!"

Some days life is nothing but a struggle to keep your head above water.

And sometimes, while struggling, carrying a new life into the world would be like
carrying a boulder out into the ocean. Both of you will only drown.

For anyone with a womb,
God built a boat and called it abortion.

He said, "You can row,
you don't have to wade out into the water and wait
for it to pull you under."

How could anyone seek to overturn that boat?

Abortion is not an issue that only affects a single gender.
There are far too many biological men speaking out against reproductive rights.
There need to be more of us speaking out for them.

HULK

A lot of people want to be superheroes.
Specifically,
a lot of biological men basically believe that their dicks are Bruce Banner.

Normally mild mannered...
and brilliant...
but if you get him aroused...
rub him the wrong way...
you end up with the Incredible Hulk – and there are no limits on his powers!

When this happens,
some men claim to lose all self-control.
And if things get a little out of hand, if they accidentally go too far,
they say they are literally not to blame for their actions when in Hulk state.

And admittedly, there is less blood in their brains.
And admittedly, I can only speak for myself.

But for me,
if someone broke into the room with a gun right at that moment,
if the house was on fire,
if there was danger of any kind...
I would still have the wherewithal to fight back,
to escape,
to try and protect anyone in the room with me.

So if you're in Hulk state and things get out of hand,
if a victim cries out and you're the aggressor,
if a woman says no and you don't stop,
then you are the gun,
you are the fire,
you are the danger.

And it's up to you to be the hero.
It's up to you to stop the Hulk.

HELP

It's just us
looking for justice in an unjust existence.
And you're in a position where you might be able to help.
So you're trying to help.
But people keep looking at you weird.
Don't stop trying to help.

You offer help without labeling it that way,
and you think you're making progress.
But still people keep questioning your motives,
and suggesting you might still be part of the problem,
and you're worried that sometimes you probably are.
Don't stop trying to help.

You realize you might only be helping out of guilt about your privilege,
and you think you're woke to what that privilege means,
but wonder if you should even be using the word, "woke," like that,
and reject the idea that you should feel guilty
about something you had no control over,
yet realize this is a classic example of a first-world problem,
and feel some cognitive dissonance over all that.
Don't stop trying to help.

You know you can't fully understand the struggles of others
without experiencing them firsthand,
but you're doing your best to understand anyway,
to support causes despite not being directly affected,
and you just got corrected for misgendering a friend.
Don't stop trying to help.

You want to get names right,
you practice pronunciation,
and still get it wrong and you just got corrected again.
Don't stop trying to to get it right.

Even you think no one sees what you do,
let alone recognizes what it means.

You aren't looking for credit,
just to not be grouped with others and labeled an enemy en masse,
and you recognize the poetic justice of that,
and even kind of revel in the turnabout,
but still wonder if it's "fair."
Don't stop trying to share your blessings.

You heard a poem that made you question whether you're helping in the right way,
or if your help is even wanted.
Don't stop trying to figure it out.

If you don't understand, ask questions.
If you think you're doing it wrong, ask questions.
If something makes you uncomfortable, ask questions.
Don't stop trying to understand.

You discover that sometimes helping means you are a ladder so someone else can climb,
a podium so someone else can speak.
Sometimes you build stages and podiums,
you build audiences and crowds,
just so someone else can speak.

You learn that sometimes helping means setting things up,
then stepping out of the way
and letting the right person's voice be heard.

You worry if any of it even matters.

And it does.

IN DEFENSE OF THE ROBBER

When the settlers first arrived in Catan,
they found a land rife with opportunity.
The terrain ranged wildly,
including endless miles of pastoral land,
perfect for growing wheat and raising sheep,
yet also thick with forests and mountain ranges,
from which they could harvest logs, bricks and ore,
to build their roads, settlements and cities.

It was practically paradise.

And yet,
in their haste to develop the apparently virginal land,
the settlers didn't consider whether anyone else might already be living there.

So when they discovered a group of indigenous people,
with darker skin and different values,
the settlers dubbed them "Robber,"
and pushed them into the center of the continent,
the least desirable piece of real estate in all of Catan:
the desert.

As settlements grew up around the desert,
the indigenous "Robbers" became pawns in a complex game between the
invaders.

The Robbers had no arms with which to defend themselves,
so moving Robbers around became the most common roll of the dice,
as each party made treaties, and then broke them,
forcing the Robbers to resettle again and again,
simply to inconvenience their neighbors.

The Robbers didn't even get to keep the resources
they supposedly "stole" from the settlers,
instead, these assets were simply returned to the bank!

And as though that wasn't insult enough,
when someone decided to create a board game
commemorating this struggle between good and evil,
they named it after the evil doers,
the Settlers of Catan,
following in the footsteps of every other historian in history,
completely rewriting the story from the settler's perspective.
And as a result, we know almost nothing about the real heroes,
the Robbers.

Most people don't know that the Robbers used to cultivate corn and raise hogs
on this land.
They don't know about the art the Robbers created or the astronomy they
practiced.
They don't know about the ceremonies the Robbers conducted or the games they
played.

And if you really want to understand a culture,
you have to look at the values in the games they play.

The settlers play games like Risk, War, Battleship and Monopoly.
In fact, they've built imperialism, capitalism and global domination into their
games so deeply,
they don't even notice it anymore.

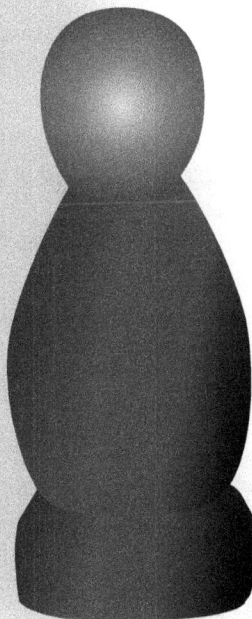

NINE PIZZAS

I was a weird kid in school in the nineties,
and the nine planets felt like better friends to me than the kids in class.

I learned my first mnemonic just to remember their names:
Mercury, Venus, Earth, Mars, Jupiter, Saturn, Uranus, Neptune, Pluto, became,
"My Very Educated Mother Just Served Us Nine Pizzas."

And I love pizza.
So this made sense to me.

In the nineties,
Star Trek and NASA teamed up to make me feel like space was right next door.

I fantasized about visiting my friends in my X-Wing!
I would see Jupiter's massive storm eye!
Venus's chemical seas!
And Pluto's ferocious... dinosaurs!

But then in 2006, they demoted Pluto from planet to dwarf planet.
And I... I thought I had lost my friend...
I've been mourning his removal from planethood for nearly a decade now.

Everything was different now:
"My Very Educated Mother Just Served Us Nine Pizzas,"
became,
"My Very Educated Mother Just Served Us Nachos."

We traded NINE pizzas for only ONE thing of nachos?
For all of us?
Just how educated is this mother anyway?

Apparently she's also been baking up new dwarf planets you've probably never
heard of:
Ceres, Haumea, Makemake and Eris.

And it wasn't just me...
there was public outcry!

Why demote Pluto!?
Was he not doing his job!?
Is it just because he's little!?

Pluto was the Roman god of the underworld.
I kept expecting the scientists who made that decision to be swallowed up by fire
and lightning,
or at least brimstone,
but it never happened.

So I've been carrying around this grudge for nine years.
And I know a lot of other people have been hurting too.

When just the other day it hit me:
I and anyone else who's still mad about Pluto has had it backwards all this time!

We didn't lose a friend,
we gained at least <u>four</u> new ones!

Just because they're small and strange,
and the other planets throw rocks at them,
and they've been hiding in the back all this time...
that doesn't mean dwarf planets aren't planets too.

It doesn't mean they don't want to be noticed.

Trust me, I used to be one of those weird kids.
And what I wanted more than anything was to be included.

Instead of being all cliquey about the eight big planets,
we should be welcoming Ceres, Haumea, Makemake and Eris into the group.

And just like that,
"My Very Excellent Mother Constantly Just Serves Us Nachos, Pizzas, Hamburgers,
Meatballs and Éclairs."

Holy Guacamole, what a feast!

And scientists think there could be hundreds more dwarf planets...
just hiding in the back...
waiting to make friends.

THRU

There once was a guru named Lou,
who lived in Timbuktu,
with a beautiful daughter named, "Thru."

Lou loved <u>two</u> things in the universe above all else:
1)   <u>His daughter, Thru</u> and 2) <u>Seeking truth</u>...

People with...

And 3) <u>Delicious pie</u>!

People with problems would come from all over the land
to gaze upon Thru and to hear Lou's wisdom,
and they always brought pie to show their appreciation.

*(Apple pie. Pecan. Chocolate pudding pie. Peach cobbler. And not just dessert
pies either, savory meat pies and deep dish pizza... chicken pot pie...)*

Now I...

(Maybe a nice quiche sometimes... pretty much anything served in a pie tin...)

Now I...

*(Though one time this guy brought Lou some cold pasta salad in a pie tin, and
Lou was like, "Come on, man. You picked this up at Whole Foods and put it in a
pie tin. There's not even a crust. I'm going to eat it because of the novelty of pasta
salad pie, but I expect a homemade pie from you next time.")*

Now I had a problem with getting stuff done.
I could never complete any tasks.
So I went to Guru Lou of Timbuktu to ask for any tips that I could have.
I brought a blueberry pie that I half-baked myself.

I told him my tale of woe and asked for his prescription.
And he said,

"Listen carefully.
For the next week, I want you to follow my daughter everywhere she goes.
In doing so,
you will learn the secret of a job well done."

And I said, "Hang on.
Follow your daughter?
Isn't that a little stalkerish?"

And he said,

> "No, no, we live in a myth! This is like, a fable.
> You're not supposed to take it literally."

And I said,
"Still, creeping around after your daughter seems a bit more Big Bad Wolf,
than Brave Lumberjack.
Just how wise are you anyway?
I heard you only moved to Timbuktu because your name is Lou.
You only live here for the rhyme!"

And he said,

> "Shut up! You aren't getting this at all! Thru, come in here!"

She entered the room like a sunrise and said,
> "What's up, Dad?"

And he said,

> "Can this guy follow you around for a few days
> until he gets the meaning of my fable?"

> "Follow me? What do you mean?"

> "It's this new thing I'm trying, I'm trying to teach this guy about following
> through. It's a wordplay on your name! 'Follow Thru,' Follow through. This whole
> thing is a set up for that. Shit, now I gave away the punchline. Look, just ignore
> him till he gets it. It won't take that long, especially 'cause I just told him."

And she said,
> "No, you look, Dad. It's bad enough that men come from all over the county to
> 'gaze upon my beauty', or whatever you want to want to call the way they
> objectify me. But now you're going to have them follow me around too? You're
> exploiting me for free pie!"

And he said,

> "That's absurd! People bring me pies because I'm wise!"

"Is that why you make me wear this uncomfortable corset every day? This is the last straw, I'm breaking out of this fable!"

Which seemed like a good time for me to leave too.
I took my half-baked pie with me.

Anyways, I never really got the point of his story.
Don't exploit your children for pie?

~ BUY ~
# DNY'S
HALF-BAKED PIES

They're
"Delicious!"

- your brain

Look for Dny's Half-Baked Pies at your favorite local retailer!

WRITING RULES

The first rule of writing is to write for yourself.
If you aren't entertained by what you write,
then what makes you think someone else would be interested in it?

However, this clashes with:
the first rule of writing is to remember your audience.

And runs parallel to the first rule of writing is that every word must be *intentional.*
Antelope sprocket.

It is very very very very very very very very very important that you are concise
and to the point.
Especially in a short poem.

And I shouldn't be talking about it because the first rule of writing is you do not
write about Write Club!
Writing about Write Club is just too meta.
Write about something else.

So the first rule of writing is to write for yourself with intention while
remembering your audience and not writing about Write Club, and being concise.

However, this clashes with,
the first rule of writing is there are no clear rules!
There's no single way to get it right.

But none of this invalidates the title of this poem...
because writing definitely rules!

AND NOW, A SONG

I don't expect to be a critical success.
Most people just don't like the stuff I write, I guess.
Yes, even when I try to do my best,
the critics look and say, "Oh my, this is a mess!"

And I think the problem is...
I'm just too smart.

                                  People don't get it!

... They're all in the dark.

                                  People don't get it!

The stuff I wrote that I thought was so great.
Was really only good enough to rate me an eight.
It's not that people hate it, they just don't care.
And in the art world, that doesn't get you – a Spoken Word Grammy!

And I think the problem is...
I'm just too smart.

                                  People don't get it!

... They're all in the dark.

                                  People don't get it!

I'm so proud of these rhyme schemes,
                          you just don't understand.
The cadence of this poem could be adapted by a band.

But I never get approached,
or offered any deals...
                    And I think everyone else must just not know how it feels...
To be this smart.

                                  People don't get it!
...I'm so damn smart.

                                  People don't get it!

I'm so smart, I'll make references
        too obscure for general audiences,
like John B. Calhoun,
        and Larry and Balki's favorite dances.

I'm so smart I have opinions, on almost anything.
From astronomy to zoology, and even how to sing.

I only corrected your grammar
and the way you pronounced that word,
but you acted so offended,
like I offered you an absurd herd of dirty nerd birds,
so you demurred and spurred me, but I was undeterred,
you deferred but slurred, so I misheard and inferred you had concurred,
so I said, "Good sir, that's not how you say 'chauffeured.'"
and it recurred a third time, so you transferred me to another department...

And I think I figured out,
the real problem now...

I'm not that smart.
                              I just don't get it!
... I live in the dark.
                              I just don't get it!

So I guess it takes real talent, to make things people like.
And if I'm going to fuck around,
and try the unexpected and break the fourth wall and standard slam format with a
ridiculous and mildly insulting song even though I can't sing,
and even not-so-subliminally suggest scores within my poem...
I guess I should expect...
to get an eight.

Or lower.

Although I would be doing myself an injustice if I didn't mention that if you really
want to reward creativity, or perhaps genuinely liked this poem, you could also
consider going in the other direction and giving me a ten.
I'm just saying.

> So here's a toast to pop,
> and things that people like,
> and to critics and judges everywhere,
> I hope you have great nights!

SONGASM (W/ ACCOMPANIMENT)

I don't know about you... but for me,
building an orgasm is a lot like singing a song.

You can't just do it on command,
you have to wait for the chorus to come around.

And sometimes it's easier to get to that chorus,
if you have accompaniment,

                              so, I need your help...

            When we get to the chorus of this poem,
                        You sing back.

                  I'm going to say,
"You just have to wait,"

and you're going to say,

                                          "for the chorus to come!"

                        Let's try it!
"Oh, you just have to wait,"

                                          "for the chorus to come!"

"Yes, you just have to wait,"

                                          "for the chorus to come!"
                        Great!

Sometimes it's a short song,
like when it's the first time you've sung in a while,
and you're just kinda testing out your vocal chords,
blowing out the dust,
                        if you will,
and there's a lot of... dust,
                        if you will,
and it just makes you want to try again as soon as you can because it's pretty
awesome, but too short, unlike this sentence I am currently speaking.

But other times, just like that amazing sentence I just spoke... it's epic.

   44

The song just goes on and on,
and you get to the point where you start to wonder if the song is going to climax at all,
or just continue building toward frustrating false crescendos,
like a fireworks show that invests so much in the build-up
                              they have nothing left for the grand finale...
so instead it just... kind of... peters out.

Now when singing solo,
this isn't usually a problem.
It's called edging, you can do it over and over again in the shower,
and it's pretty awesome!
Like the lead guitarist, keyboardist and backing vocalist for the band U2,
The Edge,
that guy with the sunglasses and beanie standing behind Bono,
he's pretty awesome too,
and all of that seems pretty appropriate when listening to "A Beautiful Day."

You can usually work it all out on your own,
and it really is a beautiful day.

But when singing a duet,
all this sometimes needs a bit of negotiation,
especially if you want to get there together,
and hit no discordant notes.
And just like The Edge,
you have to do this without completely losing the rhythm.
And you have to wear a little beanie hat while rocking out.

Either way, it helps if you have a drummer,

"And then you just have to wait,"
                                        "for the chorus to come!"

"Yes, you just have to wait,"
                                        "for the chorus to come!"

and you just have to wait for it to come back around...
And you just have to wait,

                                        "for the chorus to come!"

Sorry, that was a butt dial...
Not a booty call.
A butt dial.

LINGUISTERRIFIC

Theres a editor whom lives in my head.
Whom wants to correct that sentence.
Whom wants to correct that one two.
Whom knows the proper use of the word, "whom,"
and whom, wants me, and everyone else, to use it correctly.

(He thinks the first sentence should read,
"An editor lives in my head."
"That's cleaner and more active," says the little guy.)

Whom is absolutely right.
But whom, is also, kinda a butthole.

He constantly line edits conversation as it comes at us.

Like when Ashton Kutcher told me,
"I was bit by a poisonous snake. I'm feeling nauseous so I'm going to lay down."
This kid in my head wanted to respond with,
"You mean 'venomous.'
Things are poisonous if you can't eat them, but they're venomous if their bite is toxic.
Also, it's 'nauseated,' not 'nauseous,' and 'lie down,' not 'lay down.'"
Rather than the more appropriate response,
"Oh no! Ashton! I'll call 911!"

Or when someone misuses the word "ironic,"
this snobby kid wants to go off like a nucular bomb,
"a nuclear bomb,"
- *sigh* -

"You're going to want to correct that," says the kid.
"'Ain't' ain't a word," says the kid.
And I want to listen to him – he lives in my head.

But I keep calling him a kid 'cause he's immature.
Like, he's all booksmart, but he doesn't know much about the real world.
And in the real world, pronunciation, grammar and meaning change over time
based on usage,

48

not based on how some editor thinks they should.
"Ain't" actually is a word and has been in the dictionary for centuries, y'all.
And "y'all" is a word too.
This is literally how language evolves.
And yes, that was the proper usage of "literally," thank you,
but it shouldn't matter.
All of us with editors in our heads are having trouble seeing outside of our skulls,
and so I've devised a test we can use when presented with improper speech:
Did you understand what the speaker meant?
Yes? Then it made sense! Fuck off!

The effect of you affecting this affect
is that everyone will think you're so obsessed with being smart,
that you aren't listening to what they are saying.

Like when your neighbor says,
"Can I axe you for a cup of sugar?"
and you say,
"Do you mean, 'May I ask you for a cup of sugar'?"
You didn't give them what they were asking for.
Classist bullshit is not sugar.

Just because someone is younger or less educated in English than you,
that doesn't mean they aren't smart or don't have meaningful things to say.

There is a time and a place to correct people.
It's when you're a parent, teacher or are asked for your edits.
And you say, "How honest should I be?"
And they say, "Go crazy!"
Then you bust that red pen all over the place!

But otherwise,
I think everybody might get along better if all of us
with tiny editors whispering in our ears,
keep their elitist, ethnocentric opinions
on the proper use of words...

in our heads.

ACCENTS OF THE SOUTH

I was born in New York.
When I was two, we moved to North Carolina, where I grew to adolescence.
But then we moved again,
and I've spent the past twenty-two years living here, in Texas.

To an outside observer,
there are at least four things North Carolina and Texas are both known for:
southern hospitality, southern bigotry, southern accents and barbeque.

Southern hospitality is true, and it's great,
but it doesn't cancel out the southern bigotry...
which sucks, and we're working on it.
Both of these things exist and are very similar between the two states.

But in the case of accents and barbeque,
folks in the know know that these things are actually flavored very differently.

Ya see, N.C. BBQ is made from pork,
due to pigs being one of the state's biggest exports,
and the sauce is thin and vinegary, adding tangy textures to the savory pulled
pork.

Whereas Texas BBQ is based on beef,
with the longhorn steer being a symbol of our lone star state,
and the sauce is thicker and sweet, perfectly glazing our tender brisket and chop.

Unfortunately, in both cases, the glorious barbeque meat market is unsustainable.

In North Carolina,
pigs produce way more waste than humans and have no sewers,
so the crick contamination is reaching ever-growing proportions.

Meanwhile, in Texas,
cattle take up way more land than humans,
and we could feed millions by growing purty much anything else on that land!

In both cases, the animals eat more calories than they produce,
and contribute more to global warming than the entire auto industry.

As a result of this unsustainability,
the price of beef and pork increases by 5% annually.
Within 20 years, these kinds of meats will be luxury items.
Within our lifetime,
a normal steak or a pack of bacon could cost $50 or $100 or more.

And I don't think I could handle that, y'all.

But there is a solution!
And I realize this probably isn't where you were expecting me to go with all this,
but... we need to...
embrace... artificially... lab-grown meat.

We need our scientists to take animal tissue
and replicate the cells
with electrical stimulation to make it grow into steak and bacon,
without ever having to make a full animal at all.

And I know it sounds gross and creepy, but think about it:
No sentient animal was harmed in the making of lab grown meat.
No living, breathing being had to be raised in horrific conditions,
only to have a farmer drag it out into the real world for the first time,
look it in the eyes, then chop off its head.

Seriously,
why buy a cow when you can grow the meat for a small fee!

So, this is a call for to anyone who loves bacon, but loves the planet more.

I know bacon jokes are kinda done, but bacon itself is timeless.
It has led me to be a hypocrite with my morals when it comes to eating meat.

So keep at it scientists!
If we all work together,
we can have lab grown meat by the end of the decade!

But that's just the opinion of one guy from New York.

"New York City?
Get a rope!"

DANNY STRACK (DNY)
IS A WRITER, ARTIST AND PERFORMER

Dny is a two time national poetry slam champion in the NPS group competition as both a team member and a coach.

As a performance poet, he holds these titles: **2007 Southwest Shootout Individual Poetry Slam Champion, 2010 Austin Poetry Slam Champion, 2012 National Group Slam Champion, Coach of the 2015 National Group Slam Champion & Southern Fried Champion Teams**, and he served as **Executive Director and Slammaster of the Austin Poetry Slam** from **2011 – 2016**.

Outside of the slam world, Dny is a tech writer, graphic designer, online marketer, maze creator, juggler, circus performer, and aspiring science fiction author. He has released 12 books of original poetry, artwork and information and is the playwright of 2 fully produced and well-received works by Austin's Sky Candy Aerial Arts – **The Time Machine (2012)** & **The Circus (2013)**.

Dny teaches performance poetry workshops in primary schools and colleges and his work is frequently used by students in poetry interpretation competitions. Dny likes flowers, balloons, ice cream, time-space, humanity, history, biology, systems theory, technology, funny stuff, games, spreadsheets, love and writing. Dny is happy to be alive!

Dny was on these slam teams: **Austin Poetry Slam** *(Team Member)* – 2007, 2008 (3rd at NPS Finals), 2009 & 2010. **Austin Slam B-Sides** *(Team Member)* – 2014. **Austin Neo-Soul Slam** *(Team Member)* – 2012 (2012 National Group Champions). **Austin Poetry Slam** *(Coach / Strategist)* – 2011 (4th in Group Finals), 2013 (5th at NPS), 2014, 2015 (2015 Southern Fried Champions, 2015 National Group Champions).

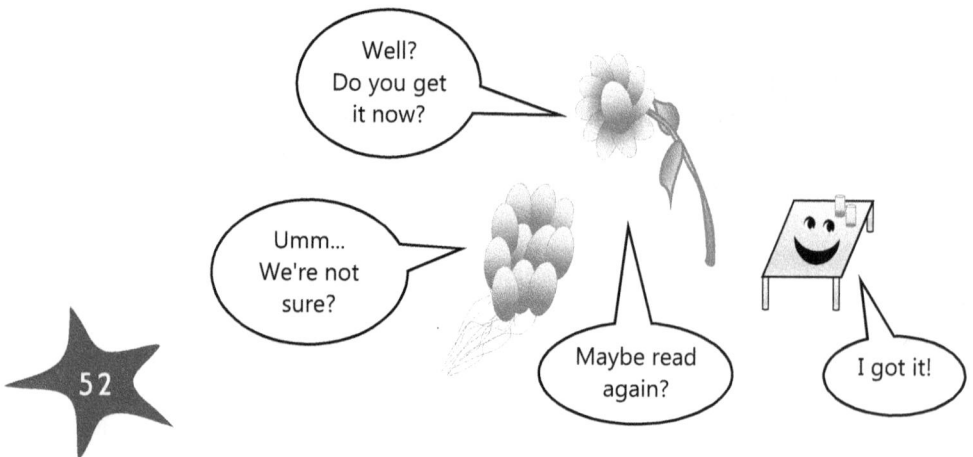

Well? Do you get it now?

Umm... We're not sure?

Maybe read again?

I got it!

52

www.ingramcontent.com/pod-product-compliance
Lightning Source LLC
Chambersburg PA
CBHW072055040426
42447CB00012BB/3129